whetstone

eira murphy

ignitionpress

First published in 2024
by **ignition**press
Oxford Brookes Poetry Centre
Oxford Brookes University
OX3 OBP

Cover design: Flora Hands, Carline Creative

A CIP record for this book is available
from the British Library

ISBN 978-1-7394543-3-3

Contents

Spring opens like a blade there.

Anne Carson, 'The Glass Essay'

Twins

In those days, we cultivated the strength of mirrors.
The terrible lie of dimension no longer echoed between us.
Instead, silver flatness, its glinted doubling that gave
no more than it promised.

Along the slow bend of light's curvature
our four-year difference, my sisterhood,
levelled itself against fresh precision.

In the upturned plastic of our bath
I watched you test out a hypothesis
of inverted return.
Beneath the water,

alive with our skin's cast off
dirt, salt, oil, the smell of turf and loch,
we tried out this logic of playing dead,

holding our breath, waiting for life to resurrect us.

My Father Skins the Rabbit

My father skins the rabbit
with a tenderness I have seen him use
for planting sweet peas in coming dusk,
fingertips running numb over stretched skin,
breaking open the stubble of an outside.

Against this transformation of pink muscle to air,
breath into stillness,
I catch my reflection in the wideness of its eye,
frame myself in dilation and capture.

Gifting my Father

I carried flowers home through the streets,
lilac leaking into the air,

kept them close to my chest,
the smell of your room held against my throat,

white bone and the sweetness of night-scented stock,
their stems chipped with water.

These flowers are for my mother
who shed her wedding ring like age from a tree.

I am giving her your body, a litany of shadows,
your mouth carved into the curve of a rose.

Anniversary

This yearly pilgrimage in search of you is like a stone
split open, capable only of revealing more of itself,
the long, mirrored journey back towards the known.

I think of your cells broken up like honeycomb,
their brittle matrices delicate as breath.
This yearly pilgrimage in search of you is like a stone.

The mountain holds your body close to its overgrown
passages and the hard ache of its silent gulf,
the long mirrored journey back towards the known.

At the hotel, three badgers with their bandit moan
reflect the dark shudder of themselves.
This yearly pilgrimage in search of you is like a stone.

My brother turns his face into a blank unknown,
reaching past the hilt of your misremembered death,
the long, mirrored journey back towards the known.

Against the sharpness of the horizon's whetstone,
I play your disappearance out across myself.
This yearly pilgrimage in search of you is like a stone,
the long, mirrored journey back towards the known.

Lanterns

She watches the darkening rim

of the park catch flame.
A thousand paper globes

pull taut against
the purpling sky,

the night like a bruise

lit up. Earth exchanges
one season for another,

the keening of summer
into autumn.

She thinks of Demeter

wreathing the world
in grief as her

daughter lies dreaming
of death. The lanterns wither

with their own heat,

speech bubbles
of skin made tender behind an ear.

Somewhere a woman is singing,
her voice unwinding itself

like string.

The lanterns falter, suspended

for a second, a bloom

of jellyfish

filling the air
with ragged flesh.

Éire

In the history books you bought me each Christmas,
   Ireland was a swan, the long whiteness of her neck
      spilling out between us,
         her black-tipped beak an arrow.

England's face was an emptiness
   or the blurred coming into focus
      of another version of time,
         uncoiling, regathering,

an endless dispersal measured out
   in salt, sickness, the hot weight of a homecoming
      illuminating all the hibernating zones of a mind
         whose protons were yet to spin out of equilibrium.

Each splintered edge of cartoon landmass
   took on the colour of a sea,
      its blue dampness, the running green of ink
         letting languages slide between letters,

the blunt glint of a ship's prow, the roil and pleat
   of landscape, its ordinary transformations redrawn,
      seen now from behind puckered glass,
         gathered and pulled out of shape.

Where did I put myself?
   In the myth of Lir, Fiachra and Conn sleep
      tucked beneath the wings of their sister
         and wait for time to release them,

their twinship a cipher for the body's tricks of disappearance,
   growing old around the silver tethering of swan-song,
      its chattering music of contract and lamellae
         falling as rain must have fallen

on emptying fields, the earth's brown thickening,
the speed and hum of machines
like overgrown cicadas or the nicotine
rasp of the natterjack calling out for love

to begin again in the swelling of spring.
Sitting in England's blanknesses,
the green and red Christmas paper seemed like a question
and as if in answer, I matched up

the nearly mirrored vowels of my name
and wondered at the accident of endings.

The Winter's Tale

On the beach, the girl is a doll.
Her mother sits on the sand as a dream
gone soft with language.
The straight line of the shore makes everything equal:
the child, the doll, the doll's mother.
This is the equation the girl draws,
pressing her fingers into the wetness of the tide.

She feels the join of her mouth,
the plastic fracture of her tongue
grow hot with doll words, disposable parts.
The sky is not above her anymore,
it is the same colour as her eyes.
She looks carefully,
her eyes and the sky form a margin.

Chop and Change Me

The boy is crouching in the belly of the tree,
his narrow feet tucked against its hollow.
Outside its polyphenolic skin
he can feel the hot rush of the axe,
its sharp predictions splicing the air.

He thinks of this severing as a song,
waking damp and panting, the hollow
thumbprint of light green skin below
his throat turned towards the axe's blade.
In his dream, the tree sets the air
ringing with its creeping undersong
of fire and bodies stretched out between tree
and boy. In the eye-dark hollow,
he realises the possibilities of his skin,
taking on the shape of the axe,
exposing their shared insides to the violence of air.

Inside, he traces the bitter cellulose of tree
against his teeth, fungus' sweetness licking up hollow
deadwood, the heady pressure of lignin lining his skin.
He has been tree for so long that the axe
might feel like liberation, a cool rush of air
unpeeling membrane from membrane, a cradlesong
to coax him from himself, picking splinters of tree
from his legs as he adjusts his eyes from hollow
dusk. He thinks of the roots left to repair
themselves and begins to match their climbing song.

Erasure

Last night, I thought about mapping the
universe onto my body in ink, letting the rain
wash me into a grey blur. This is
not enough. I want to be full
of emptiness, the breath of ghosts,
the gentle smoothness of tonight
an unbroken stillness that
mirrors us. I want to tap
into that long radio silence and
be eaten up by the blankness of a sigh.

Saint Agnes

The hard outline
of her body begins
to burn itself away,
pale flames
like glass
sprouting up
around her.

Pain comes finally
as noise,
emulsifying
like fat spheres
of oil
suspended in water,
regrouping after
each shock of movement.

Fire forces her
into the first person
and she remembers
her mother
softening the grooves
of her skin
with butter,
the smell of it turning
green in afternoon heat.

Once, she watched
a stork
pull its nest apart,
letting its four eggs
break open
as they fell.

She gathered up
the branches and prayed
over them,
letting the match
taunt their edges
leaving behind
a raised spoor
of blisters.

In her memory,
the eggs
are nothing
more than
tapered shell
and the fullness
of an outline.

On a white page,
she hollows out
a sentence.
She can feel it
crouched beneath
her tongue,
its syllables
nestled together
like grapes.

Psalter

I've this recent dream of us turned
to paper and lost somewhere to the thick
mucus of a watersoaked earth,
your chin locked against my neck
giving way to shoulder blade and clavicle,
the clumsiness of movement
recast in iron gall.

In the dream, you taste the same,
the familiar light touch of soap
mixing with the way a body smells after sleep,
at once delicate and feral.

It suits us, this lack of dimension,
the way the dreaming mind converts us
into a neatly folded quire,
simplifying our attachment.

Connemara

All day the globing blue of sky and sea
tucked like two growing bodies into one another,

a muddle of foetal legs and arms,
the salt-cure of new skin.

Amidst this landscape, I redrew the territories
of my own creatureliness,

a muscular cartography
that let animal and shoreline

bloom fresh against the human,
the body an arena for something else.

Years ago, did we stand here differently,
younger or perhaps more precise,

smelling of seaweed, the glitter-grit of sand
like late afternoon stubble on a throat,

throwing our arms wide against it all,
a shared geography of twice-mended bones

and unhatched teeth.
I have loved all these faultlines

as one might think to love
some other small roosting thing,

tracing them fresh each morning,
each part of me a hinge into feeling.

Red-legged Partridge

When disturbed, it prefers to run rather than fly

O partridge! Bloody-footed
Lady Macbeth on her hands and knees,
the clumsy trace of martyrdom setting the snow aflame.
At the breakfast table, I imitate your soft cluck,
the thrill of *bird* emptying out my bones.

I have made you my companion this winter,
imagining the feathered boon of your breast
against mine, the ferric glint of beak and eye.
I make a nest for your clutch of eggs,
watch you settle over them with the dank heat
of parenthood, crooning over each pale birthmark,

and fashion myself a wing from old bedsheets,
wrap its length around me,
corseted like a winding sheet
or the swaddling cloths made to tame limbs
to the cruel demands of gravity
and the wet stink of earth.

Disgrace

From where I stood it could have been anything.
Death had not yet occurred to me.
I thought first of the waxed limbs
of children's toys and painted skin,
synthetic flesh with ready-made muscle.

Closer though, and the small accusatory
body of the pig came into view,
its pink rigor mortis curing the air
with the smell of animal and plastic.
Against the green edge of the bin,
its trotter, like two burnt thumbs,
announced the curled slump of its head.
The pig's face no longer looked like a pig,
reduced to the outline of a creature.
I held my own arms out as if to double it,

compared our nakedness,
and was reminded of that lost Wednesday,
our bodies thickened with sleep,
the backs of your legs jutting out from the sheets,
upturned and greased with light,
how hungry I'd felt at the sight of them.

Passions

For Roe

With rabbit
between her teeth,
Joanna tells me to have grace
and begins to decipher
the rehearsed mysteries
of the body,
its movements
strung up against the shallow night
as shadow play.
I listen to the green breaking
of a river,
the pit of me
churning like furious earth.
I read about the slicing
of children's hearts,
what privacy they hold.
I read about the small passions
and feel myself
fill with their red creatures
creeping love and forest into me.

I am full of static and she says
there is a picture there
if only you can reach out
and feel the edges of it
curl like lit paper.
I would like to be fire,
or the failure to burn,
an invisibility to pin your hopes to
in the stuttering of a mammal's chest.
I can hold all this apart from myself,
collapse around it.
O Joanna,
I can be like an echo and find my way back towards
the sound of my own voice like moths

loosening themselves in light,
eating their way through old carpet and desire,
drunk on the stillness of a direction.

The Foundling Museum

In this mirroring that loosens
me from myself in the shock of exhibition glass,
the milky outline of my face dissolving
under the museum's white light
is another object
in rows of ribbon, halved medallions,
tin fists worn to ward off loneliness
and safety pinned as memory.

Here I might sit on the edge of a bed and finish up
the story you began elsewhere,
your mother with her hands boiled crimson under soap and water
watching you jump from a bedroom window,
the split-second lie of flight catching at your hair.

I might summon you back mid-sentence,
language pulling at the corners of your mouth
like some ventriloquist's doll,
and let you tell me how you crept soundlessly
each evening towards the sea, a pale blur against the coastline,
and willed yourself towards him,
the cliff edge a meniscus
or a muscle in an arm viewed beneath its layers of skin.

In the museum, I pull you in and out of view,
a magic trick or the lining up of compass points,
watch our faces group and regroup
in the tremors of reflection.

Ebbinghaus Forgetting Curve

For Rua

I can still hear a horse crying out,
its wild scream unspooling
along the thin vein of a morning.
I hold the metal pain of its voice
between us and the Spanish street
with its smell of petrol and cooling rubber,
the silver gleam of the sea like a wave of frequency.

I picture you at twenty-four slicing
apple peel into ribbons at an open window
and wonder how it felt to watch
the dry heat of the day curdle into night,
a new awareness of the earth's pull and sway
tugging at your throat.

I wonder if you gave yourself a year
to forget, tracing the unlooping
of the engram cells from their circuit
across the soft skin of a wrist,
the white ridges of a back
stretched flat against a bed,
if you thought of this process
as balloons cut loose
from one another,

drifting slowly out towards an invisible point.

Notes

'Chop and Change Me' takes for its title a line from John Lyly's play, *Love's Metamorphosis*.

'Erasure' incorporates a line from Edna St. Vincent Millay's 'What lips my lips have kissed, and where, and why'.

'Red-legged Partridge' takes for its epigraph a line from the Wikipedia article on red-legged partridges.

Acknowledgements

Thank you to the *Oxford Review of Books* for publishing an earlier version of 'Disgrace'.

With much love and thanks to: Lydia Ciaccio for being my through line, Roe Rajah, Judith Palmer, Sarah Corbett, Simon and Jennie Craske, Samera Naji, Teja Jingree, Indira Matta, Maddie O'Connor Manson, Eliza Browning, and Han Au Chua, by whom I feel so lucky to be known; and to Kas Pietrzak for the postcards and the Szymborska. With particular thanks to Niall Munro for his editorial guidance; and to Susannah Rose.

These words are for Deryn and Felix, for Michael and Brenda. All the way round and back again.

MIX
Paper from
responsible sources
FSC® C007326
FSC
www.fsc.org

Oxford Brookes is committed to the environment.
This document is printed using processes that are:

100% Net Carbon Negative
100% Renewable Energy
100% ISO14001
100% eco-friendly simitri® toner
100% Recyclable Stock

Zero% waste to landfill

Printed by seacourt – proud to be counted amongst the top environmental printers in the world